# TOOTH
*AND*
## CLAW

Grizzly bear track
in the sand.
(about ½ life-size)

# TOOTH
## AND
# CLAW

## Animal
## Adventures
## in the Wild

## Ted Lewin

**HarperCollins**Publishers

## Also by Ted Lewin

*Big Jimmy's Kum Kau Chinese Take Out*

*Red Legs: A Drummer Boy of the Civil War*

*Gorilla Walk*

*Elephant Quest*

*Peppe the Lamplighter*
by Elisa Bartone

*Market!*

*The Day of Ahmed's Secret*
by Florence Parry Heide and Judith Heide Gilliland

*Fair!*

Library of Congress Cataloging-in-Publication Data
Lewin, Ted.
Tooth and claw : animal adventures in the wild / Ted Lewin.— 1st ed.
p.     cm.
Summary: Author-illustrator Ted Lewin relates fourteen of his experiences
with wild animals while traveling the world, following each anecdote with
facts about the featured animal and its habitat.
ISBN 0-688-14105-6 — ISBN 0-688-14106-4 (lib. bdg.)
1. Wildlife watching—Juvenile literature.   2. Dangerous animals—Juvenile literature.   3. Lewin, Ted—Jouneys—Juvenile
literature.   [1. Wildlife watching.   2. Dangerous animals.   3. Animals—Habits and behavior.
4. Lewin, Ted.   5. Voyages and travels.]   I. Title: Tooth and claw.   II. Title.
QL60 .L5   2003   590—dc21   2002004588

1 2 3 4 5 6 7 8 9 10
❖
First Edition

To my wife, Betsy, who shares all of life's adventures with me.

Porcupine quills
Kalahari

Special thanks to James G. Doherty, Vice President and General Curator of Wildlife, Wildlife Conservation Society/Bronx Zoo.

NY-London

NY-Brussels

NY-Frankfurt

Frankfurt—New Delhi Long trip.

Can see the Pyramids from the air.

By car to Kanha N.P. Pandias in hills!

London—Cairo—Nairobi—(Kampala)
(8,300 miles)

Cairo

NY-Johannesburg.
Very long trip.

(14)

(7)

Nairobi

(4) (12)

Bumpy flight over Lake Victoria in a British Comet airplane.

Long, dusty drive.

Rough trip by van.
Flooded roads.
Get stuck many times.

Johannesburg—Gaborone.
Many hours by Bedford Truck
into the Kalahari. Hard trip.
Arrive Roger's Pan after dark.

(6)

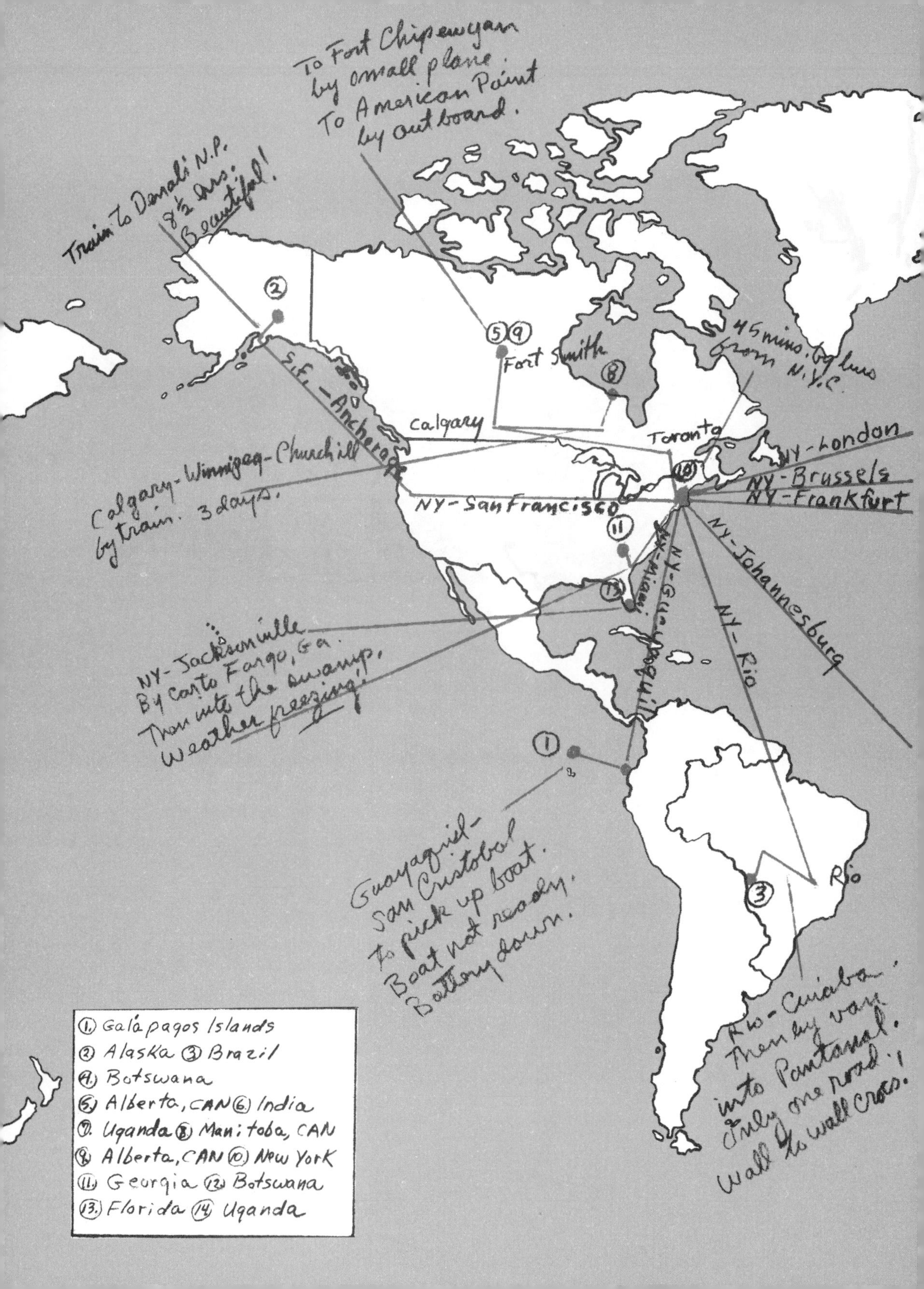

To Fort Chipewyan
by small plane
To American Point
by outboard.
Train to Denali N.P.
8½ hrs.
Beautiful!
Fort Smith
45 mins. by bus
from N.Y.C.
S.F.—Anchorage
Calgary
Toronto
NY-London
NY-Brussels
NY-Frankfurt
Calgary-Winnipeg-Churchill
by train. 3 days.
NY-San Francisco
NY-Johannesburg
NY-Miami
NY-Rio
NY-Jacksonville
By car to Fargo, Ga.
Then into the swamp.
Weather freezing!
Guayaquil-
San Cristobal
to pick up boat.
Boat not ready.
Battery down.
Rio
Rio-Cuiaba.
Then by van
into Pantanal.
Only one road.
Wall to wall crocs!
1. Galápagos Islands
2. Alaska 3. Brazil
4. Botswana
5. Alberta, CAN 6. India
7. Uganda 8. Manitoba, CAN
9. Alberta, CAN 10. New York
11. Georgia 12. Botswana
13. Florida 14. Uganda

# Contents

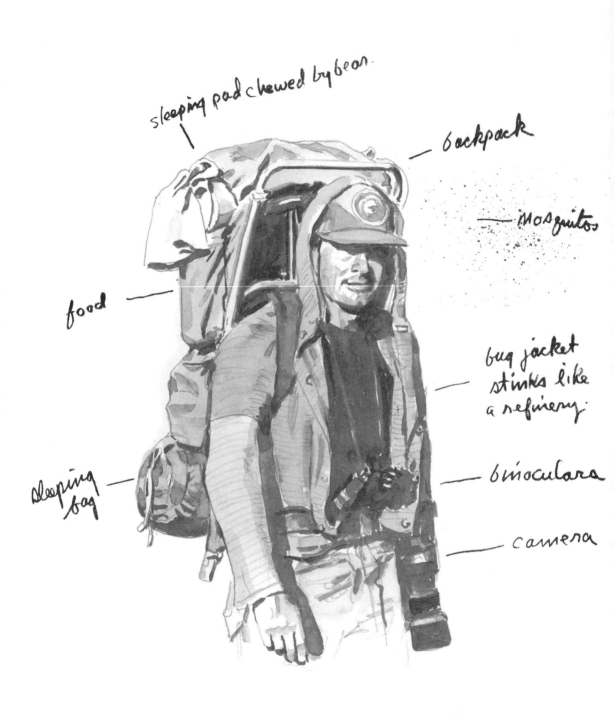

sleeping pad chewed by bear

backpack

mosquitos

food

bug jacket
stinks like
a refinery

sleeping
bag

binoculars

camera

# Foreword

I've often been asked how these journeys come about. Whenever my wife,

Betsy, and I get the urge to travel, we phone our friends in Germany, Bodo

and Waltraut Szonn, and together, we make plans. Sharing the expenses

allows us to do things none of us could afford to do on our own: rent a

plane or a private charter boat, or hire a special guide. Many months and

phone calls later, we meet in some very strange places: a rug souk (market)

in Marrakesh or the maharajah's palace in Madras. And, at

journey's end, we part in even stranger places: a pool hall in Winnipeg or

a lavu (tipi) in Lapland.

The stories here are told from my point of view, but for the most part,

they are based on memories of our shared experiences.

# GALÁPAGOS ISLANDS, ECUADOR

Oldest of the islands.
3,000,000 years old.

Hood Island

Where I saw
the boobies.

INNREIST
2 5 MAR 1991
PASSKONTROLLEN
FORNEBU

PARQUE NACIONAL
DIRECCIÓN NACIONAL FORESTAL
ECUADOR
GALÁPAGOS

blue-footed
booby

ILUSTRE MUNICIPALIDAD DEL CENTRO
SAN CRISTOBAL
GALÁPAGOS-ECUADOR
Nº 1957

TARJETA DE A

REPUBLICA DEL ECUADOR
TARJETA DE INGRESO A PARQUES NACIONALES
Y RESERVAS EQUIVALENTES

Nombre
Agencia Trans
Fecha de entra

Valor de la Especie

¿Equivalente d

Alcalde

REPUBLICA DEL ECUADOR
TARJETA DE INGRESO A PARQUES NACIONALES
Y RESERVAS EQUIVALENTES

# 1 / Beach Master

I watched as the bull sea lion patrolled just off Hood Island. I could hear his throaty, coughlike bark. It was August and close to breeding season. These bulls—at six hundred pounds, bigger than Hulk Hogan and The Rock combined—were fighting over the best beaches for their harems. So far, this beach seemed to be unclaimed.

It was the second week of island hopping in the Galápagos Islands on an old tub called *The Poderoso*. My guide, William, and I came ashore in a panga, riding the big blue-green Pacific rollers. It had been a wet trip. I was worried about my cameras, hoping

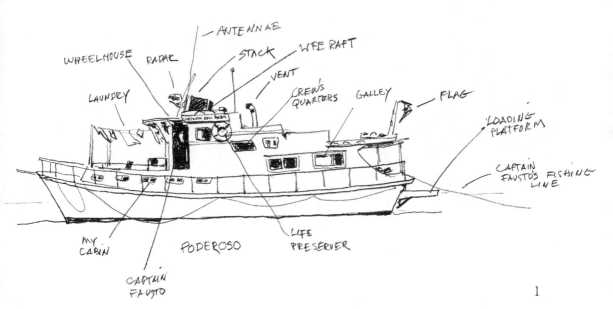

ANTENNAE

WHEELHOUSE  RADAR  STACK  LIFE RAFT

VENT

LAUNDRY  CREW'S QUARTERS  GALLEY  FLAG

LOADING PLATFORM

CAPTAIN FAUSTO'S FISHING LINE

MY CABIN  PODEROSO  LIFE PRESERVER

CAPTAIN FAUSTO

dancing

clicking bills

P.U.!

I can hardly breathe!

the waterproof bags had kept them dry.

As we beached the panga, I looked around. Blue-footed boobies were nesting and dancing on the ground so close together, I could hardly pick my way through them. I could barely breathe either because of the strong smell of their droppings. The boobies had no fear of humans, just like all the other animals I had encountered in the Galápagos. I had swum with friendly sea lions and sat among crowds of marine iguanas. Now, frigate birds wheeled overhead like flying dragons. William took off his goofy black straw fedora and waved them off. I hated that hat.

The hat.

"Nice hat, William," I said sarcastically the first time I saw it. William was very meticulous about his attire, but his goofy hat made no sense. It wasn't a proper guide hat. It was a dress hat. It undermined my confidence in him.

Every day, William wore a clean, starched uniform, the goofy hat, but no shoes. One day I saw him walking barefoot on razor-sharp lava rocks.

"How can you stand it?" I asked.

"Indigenous feet," he replied.

William was highly trained as a Galápagos guide. He constantly worked on improving his English by asking the meaning of certain words. One day, on *The Poderoso*, he asked the meaning of the word *capsize*.

_— the hat!_

*Why does he need to know* that? I wondered.

Now we walked carefully through the colony of blue-footed boobies. We came to a deserted beach where the bull sea lion swam offshore. I began to photograph him with my telephoto lens. I could see him very clearly and up close through the lens. The bull

_— indigenous feet_

swam back and forth beyond the waves, finally turning in toward shore. He started getting bigger in the lens as he surfed in like a bullet on the breakers.

I snapped away. He came through the spume right up onto the beach, waddling on his front flippers, filling my camera frame completely.

*Snap! Snap!* It was then that I noticed that all I saw was his head and horny crest looking right into the lens at me. He didn't look happy.

I lowered the camera. The angry bull, mouth wide open and full of teeth like an attack dog, foot-long whiskers bristling, was just ten feet from me and coming at full tilt. My heart leaped and I turned to run, expecting at any moment to lose a large chunk of my rear end. My foot caught in the soft sand and I twisted my knee. As I ran, limping painfully, I saw William leap in between us, flailing his hat to distract the sea lion. The sea lion veered off and went for the hat. He apparently didn't like it any better than I did.

William made a couple of nifty open-field moves, feinting toward the left, then moving quickly to the right and out of danger. He sauntered back to me now, wearing his hat at a particularly annoying angle. I said, "William, I *really* like that hat."

A few days later when we said our good-byes back on Santa Cruz, where our journey began, I gave William a pair of my sneakers for his "indigenous" feet. He offered his hat in trade.

The hat again!

Waves exit through a hole in the lava and shoot 150 feet into the air. Spectacular!

Blowhole

# AUTHOR'S NOTE

The Galápagos Islands lie six hundred miles off the coast of Ecuador in the Pacific Ocean. They are volcanic in origin, and some of the volcanoes are still active. Until 1539 the islands were inhabited only by animals. The five largest islands are Isabela, Santa Cruz, San Cristóbal, Fernandina, and San Salvador. They are home to many kinds of land- and seabirds and animals. Some of them, such as the giant tortoise, marine iguanas, and flightless cormorants, are found nowhere else in the world.

California sea lions live in herds. Each herd consists of a group of females and pups, and a bull called a beach master, who fiercely guards his territory. The males are much bigger than the females—up to seven feet long. Sea lions eat fish, octopus, and squid.

Frigate birds have a wingspan of almost eight feet and a scissorlike tail. The males are identified by a bright red throat patch, which they inflate to attract females.

5

ALASKA, U.S.

Denali National
Park

Denali!

I'm two
cars back.

# 2/Grizzly

Denali! At 20,320 feet, Denali, also known as Mount McKinley, is the highest mountain in Alaska, or anywhere in the United States. I watched it right out there, framed by the window of my railroad car, snow-capped and gleaming in the sun. I was lucky. Clouds usually hide it, and most visitors never get to see it.

I was taking a winding, eight-and-a-half-hour train trip from Anchorage to Denali National Park, where I'd planned to hike and camp for ten days. At the park station I grabbed my backpack from the baggage car. The pack weighed forty pounds. It held a tent, ground sheet, sleeping bag, rubber mat, freeze-dried food, stove, and extra clothes. I headed for the Visitors' Center to get a backcountry permit that would allow me to camp deeper inside the park.

She's faster — than she looks.

The first things I saw were these warning signs:

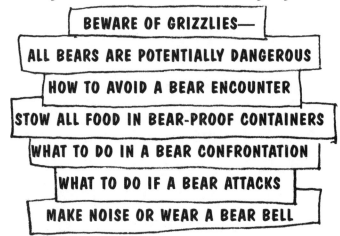

**BEWARE OF GRIZZLIES—**

**ALL BEARS ARE POTENTIALLY DANGEROUS**

**HOW TO AVOID A BEAR ENCOUNTER**

**STOW ALL FOOD IN BEAR-PROOF CONTAINERS**

**WHAT TO DO IN A BEAR CONFRONTATION**

**WHAT TO DO IF A BEAR ATTACKS**

**MAKE NOISE OR WEAR A BEAR BELL**

Now, thoroughly bear-shy, I decided to rethink getting that backcountry permit. I boarded the old school bus that took you on the only road through the park. At Teklanika campsite, I got off and set up my tent. Remembering the warning sign, I stowed my food in the bear-proof containers. Finally I was ready to take a short hike.

I felt that I would be safe if I stayed close to the campsite.

— Mama

I walked a trail that cut through a stand of willows alongside the steep bank of a glacial torrent, milky blue-white and ice-cold. It let out onto open tundra that was thick with blueberry bushes.

Three dark bear shapes

_— uh-oh!_

materialized out of the glaring disk of the sun, now low on the horizon. The largest was the size of a refrigerator. She had a golden halo on her shoulders, the grizzle of a grizzly bear. A mother and two half-grown cubs were coming steadily my way.

I couldn't go back into the willow thicket. That's where the bears were headed. I couldn't climb down the steep bank behind me into the glacial rush. I'd never make it across. I wanted to run, but I had no place to go. So, I stood still and waited.

A strange passivity came over me. I couldn't swallow. I stopped breathing. I was terrified, frightened more by what I

9

knew of the grizzly's fierce reputation than by Big Mama over there, chomping down on the branches and scraping blueberries into her mouth with a sweep of her head. The cubs stuck to her sides like Velcro, gobbling fallen blueberries. I remained rooted to the ground. My knees began to give way.

The bears passed directly in front of me. I still had no place to go. They acted as if I weren't there, feeding as they came. They passed within twenty-five feet of me and headed into the thicket.

Just before she moved out of sight, Big Mama turned her huge head and looked right at me. The cubs scurried on. Perhaps she had gotten my scent and had known I was there all the while. My heart pounded so hard, it hurt my ears. Big Mama turned. She was gone.

I couldn't move from that spot for five long minutes. I still shook all over. But now I found myself grinning foolishly: If I'd worn my bear bell, I might not have seen the grizzlies at all.

Not a bear in sight!

# AUTHOR'S NOTE

There are forty thousand grizzlies in Alaska, more than in any other state in the United States. Grizzlies are immensely strong animals with sicklelike claws for digging and slashing. Their eyesight is similar to that of humans. They eat fruit, small mammals, fish, and even seaweed. Grizzlies that live along the coast and feed on salmon grow to huge sizes, as high as ten feet tall, and weigh up to fifteen hundred pounds—as much as ten average-size men.

About two hundred grizzlies live in Denali. They eat mostly a vegetarian diet and reach a weight of approximately seven hundred pounds. All grizzly cubs weigh only a pound or so at birth.

Grizzlies hibernate. In winter they retire to a den, enter a state of deep sleep, and remain inactive until spring.

Denali is a subarctic wilderness larger than Massachusetts. Besides grizzlies, 36 species of mammals make their home there, from lynx and moose to snowshoe hare and caribou, as well as 130 bird species, including the golden eagle. Within it are stands of spruce and willow shrubs, tussock grass, moist tundra, and, at higher elevations, alpine tundra.

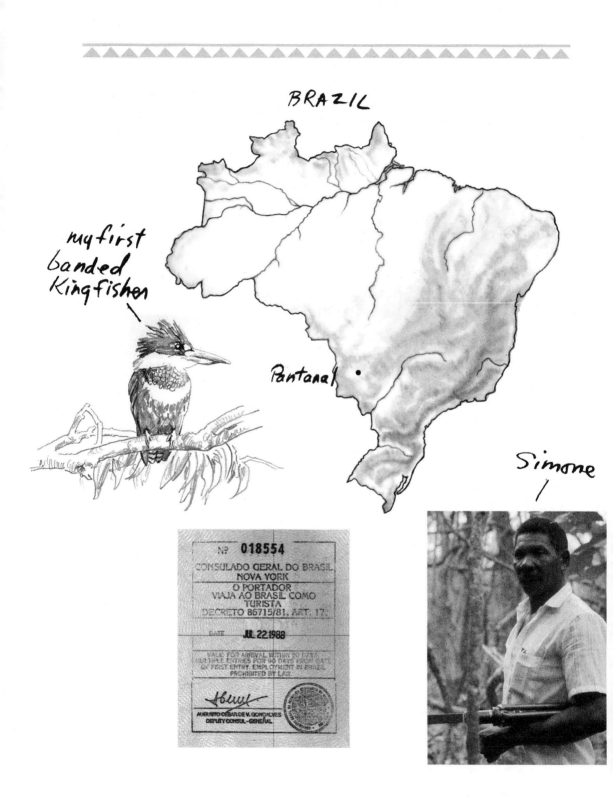

BRAZIL

my first
banded
Kingfisher

Pantanal •

Simone

NP **018554**
CONSULADO GERAL DO BRASIL
NOVA YORK
O PORTADOR
VIAJA AO BRASIL COMO
TURISTA
DECRETO 86715/81, ART. 17.

DATE   **JUL 22 1988**

VALID FOR ARRIVAL WITHIN 90 DAYS,
MULTIPLE ENTRIES FOR 90 DAYS FROM DATE
OF FIRST ENTRY. EMPLOYMENT IN BRAZIL
PROHIBITED BY LAW.

AUGUSTO CESAR DE V. GONÇALVES
DEPUTY CONSUL-GENERAL

# 3 / Macaco Meojor

I had left the little cow town of Cuiabá at the edge of the Pantanal in western Brazil in a four-wheel drive. The back of the van was loaded with plastic jugs full of extra gas. I had been told by an old hand that there were no gas stations along the road until you reached Santa Rosa on the Cuiabá River, and you couldn't make it there on one tank.

The only road into the Pantanal is built up on a ten-foot-high dike and crosses one hundred rough wooden bridges. In the wet season, it is barely above water. Now, in the dry season, it was a platform from which I could view a wildlife spectacle that rivals the Serengeti Plain of Africa with its sheer numbers of animals, countless South American caimans, or jacares, birds, fish, snakes, rodents, and all sorts of other creatures.

The first bit of civilization I came to was a little hacienda called Beira Rio. I pulled off the road past a nesting pair of Joao

John of the mud nest

dining room

My room

panga

de barrio, or John of the mud birds. They build tiny little dome-shaped mud houses to nest in.

I drove to the front of the hotel, checked in, and left my gear in the room. It was siesta time, so I went out on the veranda and sank into a hammock. The hammock enveloped me, swallowing me whole. In the sag, my backside almost touched the ground. Around the hammock, yellow-tailed caciques and tiny, red-and-black cardinals picked at scraps. The smallest of the round-bellied pigs that ran loose around the compound sniffed and rooted beneath me.

Simone woke me. It was late afternoon. I swung my legs over the side of the hammock and sat up groggily. Simone was a huge black-skinned Brazilian with a thick neck, broad shoulders, and hands as large as

z z z z Z Z Z Z Z Z

hams. I had noticed him feeding the pigs when I first arrived. He cupped his ear with his hand. Taking his cue, I listened and heard a storm brewing somewhere—a vague, drifting in and out thunder.

Simone said, "Macaco meojor" (ma-KAH-ko myor). I didn't speak Portuguese, so I had no idea what he meant. He pointed to a red aluminum panga down in the river and motioned for me to follow him.

We got into the panga, and Simone began to paddle upstream. Paddling was hard work. Dense jungle pushed in on both banks. The current seemed sluggish, but Simone was working mightily against it. His forehead glistened with beads of sweat, and his huge shoulder muscles were taut against his wet shirt.

The storm seemed to

be getting closer. Simone pointed ahead toward the sound and repeated, "Macaco meojor." I still didn't understand what he meant.

A sun bittern waded in a shady backwater. If only he would have spread his wings and shown me the sunburst of colorful feathers hidden beneath.

The sound became louder with each bend in the river. It was unnerving. I realized it was not an approaching storm. Now it sounded like the roar of an enormous engine rising, *Open wide. Teeth inside!* and then falling. I couldn't pin it down.

A big jacare sunned on the sand flats, mouth agape, oblivious to the sound. A pair of capybaras, ninety-pound rodents, sparred

# World's biggest rats!

on the riverbank and disappeared into the jungle. We came upon the carcass of a swamp deer, the juices oozing from its open belly like wet black mud. It was covered with emerald green flies. Big long-tailed birds called chachalacas cried in the distance, sounding like deranged people.

The storm sound now rolled up and down in decibels that made my insides tremble. I could barely concentrate on anything else. It was disorienting.

"Macaco meojor," Simone yelled over the roar.

Simone ran the boat into a dense thicket on the bank. We climbed out into a tunnel in the jungle full of tangled and twisted vines. I ducked and squirmed through the underbrush, trying to keep Simone in sight. The sound intensified. Now it was painful.

Simone pointed up. The tree canopy shook wildly.

Then suddenly the trees were still and there was *no* sound. Zip. Simone smiled at me and whispered almost reverently, "Macaco meojor!"

*Oookay*, I thought, *Macaco meojor means something that's loud enough to break your eardrums, but is invisible.*

Back at the hacienda, I fished out my field guide to South American animals. A macaco meojor is a red howler monkey.

# AUTHOR'S NOTE

At three feet tall, a red howler monkey is one of the largest of the New World monkeys. It has reddish brown fur and a prehensile tail. All male howler monkeys are known for their incredibly loud calls, made by specialized larynxes and jaws. The males lead troops of six to eight monkeys. To defend their territories, they shout for long periods at rival troops. They can be heard from almost two miles away. Once you hear the sound of howlers, it remains fixed in your memory. There's nothing else like it in nature.

In Brazil there is a marsh the size of Pennsylvania. It is called Pantanal, which means "big swamp" in Portuguese. In the wet season rivers overflow their banks, flooding the plains and making islands of the forest patches. The water recedes in the dry season, leaving ponds and streams that trap millions of fish. Birds, jacares, and other wild creatures gather in huge numbers to feast on this windfall and sometimes on one another. The Pantaneiros fish with pole or bow and arrow from dugout canoes.

Mercury pollution from gold mining, pesticides from soybean farming, deforestation, and poaching all pose serious threats to this natural wonder.

BOTSWANA

Central Kalahari
Game Reserve

my
camp

wide-open spaces!

# 4 / Waiting for a Puff Adder

Kalahari. The name hints of mystery. Wild. Hard. Vast. It is the largest area of sand in the world, extending across three countries: Botswana, South Africa, and Namibia. There are no roads, and because of the heat and the lack of water, it is inhabited by only a few bands of hunter-gatherer Bushmen and wild animals.

Perhaps it is the vastness that makes one do strange things. Perhaps it is the desolation. Perhaps this is why I'm sitting here by the desiccated carcass of a hartebeest, waiting for a puff adder. I wonder what it's doing down in its hole. Maybe it isn't even *in* its hole.

Yesterday I had walked a short distance from fly camp, my temporary tented camp, to sketch the carcass. It was too hot to go on a game drive. All the animals were resting in the shade, waiting for it to cool down, as I should have been.

I sat down and began sketching. The poor hartebeest had probably died of brand siekte, the sunburnlike disease that had weakened and killed so many hartebeests that year.

It was quiet and still. The only sound was the rasping movement of my pencil on the paper. It was more than ninety degrees, even though the sun had long since dropped from directly overhead and the rays now beat down at a slant. I sketched away, intent on my project, sweat wetting the crown of my bush hat.

In the deep silence I heard the sound of something dragging across the sand, a scraping, scratching sound that was barely audible. There on the soft sand, a puff adder glistened.

I gasped and stopped breathing. It's rare to see a snake in the wild. I'd only seen snakes twice before, and never a puff adder. It

*Watch your step !*

was three feet long and as fat in the middle as a yellow-green overstuffed sausage. It had an ominous, squat, triangular head and wide-set bead eyes. It undulated slowly to within six inches of my foot and stopped. I was mesmerized.

Why do things that crawl on their bellies have this effect on humans? We marvel at their beauty, and at the same time we are repulsed by their cold stare and slithery movements.

The snake turned and moved away, crawling under the branches of a Terminalia bush. I started breathing again. I got up and slowly approached it. I was determined to get a closer look. I wished I had brought my camera. The back of the puff adder was covered with diamond shapes that looked like Bushman beadwork. It crawled into the center of the bush and suddenly dropped from view. Gone in an instant. The only thing I could see was its burrow in the sand.

So, here I sit, waiting, this time with my camera. There are enormous, towering thunderheads in the sky. The silence is profound, broken only by the buzzing flies and the happy chirping of the tiny scaled finches. Above the pan nearby, two kestrels cry at each other, touch wing tips, flip over, touch talons, and fly off like speeding bullets.

Where is my scaly friend? It may not be in the same place. I remind myself to be careful. Puff adders are ill-tempered and extremely venomous. Worst of all, they're sluggish, which accounts for them being stepped on so much.

I remember that I haven't looked behind me for a while. I turn very slowly. No puff adder. I look at my watch. It's four twenty P.M. I've been here an hour. I look hard into the bush where I last saw my legless friend. I wait some more. Maybe I conjured up the snake yesterday in the heat. Then I think, *No, I couldn't have invented seeing that creature. I've got to get a picture of it.*

I know he's down there in his hole where it's cool. He's way smarter than I.

It's so still. An immense stillness. Here I sit in the middle of the Kalahari, an area bigger than California, and wait at one small bush. I feel like a kid on Christmas Eve. What am I doing?

Then it hits me. The chance of a puff adder reappearing is as likely as lightning striking twice in the same place. I get up. My legs are stiff from sitting so long. I'm slightly woozy from the heat.

As I walk back to camp, it suddenly occurs to me that the snake *could* be in the tall grass, just waiting for me to step on it.

Thunderheads

# AUTHOR'S NOTE

The Kalahari gets enough rain to make it a semiarid region but not a true desert like the Sahara. It is well vegetated with tall grasses, open woodland, scrubland, and mature forests. It has dry riverbeds and seasonal pans. A pan is a natural depression in the sand with a floor of hard clay. When it rains, it fills up and becomes a source of water for animals. Salts collect when the water evaporates. Animals will dig at the surface to get at the salt, which is a necessary part of their diet. Animals may survive without water by drinking from plants wet with dew. They also eat buried tubers, swollen with moisture, a favorite of the Bushmen as well.

Puff adders are found almost everywhere in Africa. They are one of the largest of the adders. They can grow to be as wide as a baseball, and as long as two baseball bats, front end to back end. Puff adders lie in wait for prey, using their color as camouflage. They eat mice, rats, birds, lizards, frogs, and toads, and will bite humans if stepped upon. They can inflate themselves to a much larger size when ready to strike.

A puff adder has two hollow half-inch-long fangs that fold back when its mouth is closed. The fangs swing forward when its mouth is wide open. Venom is pumped from a venom gland at the base of the fang and injected as the fangs puncture the snake's victim. A puff adder carries enough venom to kill four or five human adults. The venom causes severe tissue damage and bleeding. Because of its wide distribution and deadly venom, it probably kills more people than any other African snake.

# ALBERTA, CANADA

license plate

NORTHWEST TERRITORIES
4·945
CANADA 1981

CUSTOMS
IMMIGRATION
DOUANES
IMMIGRATION
9 VII 1984
TORONTO
245

Wood Buffalo
National Park

Eyes and ears

Not —
so
good.

—— Nose, very good!

# 5/Bears, Bears, Bears

My week in Alberta, Canada, was almost over. I had been camped at Sweetgrass Station in Wood Buffalo National Park. I had seen an old bull bison, alone and dangerous, a pure white wolf, and a cross fox. There were beavers, woodchucks, barn owls, bald eagles, and bears, bears, bears.

A week earlier Orville Big Legs, a Cree Indian guide, brought me upriver in his aluminum skiff. On the hike in, I'd scared off a half dozen black bears by yelling and clapping at them. Once, while skinny-dipping in Sweetgrass Creek, I was flanked by bears feeding on both banks. I stood in the middle of the creek, naked and shivering, until they left.

Now it was time to rendezvous with Orville on the Peace River.

I reluctantly slipped on my head and body net. It looked like chain mail and was soaked with insect repellent. The repellent worked wonders against the conquering hordes of hungry mosquitoes, but it didn't stop their incessant buzzing, and it stank like a refinery. Without it I would've been eaten alive on the half-day's walk back to the rendezvous point.

I passed the rotting old corrals and entered the narrow, overgrown trail. It had been an old wagon road, used to bring loads of hay to the bison corralled here. In 1965 the Canadian government used helicopters to round up the bison for inoculation against the infectious disease anthrax. It is caused by a bacterium and is usually fatal to cattle and sheep. In 1978 they stopped inoculations because so many bison died from the stress of the roundup.

I walked along contemplating the bison when a black bear

*Alone and dangerous!*

28

I don't hear any bells.

appeared up ahead on the trail. I yelled, and it fled into the woods. After my grizzly experience in Alaska, I was more bearwise and knew what to do. If you come upon bears, make noise, let them know you're there, scare them off.

I was in black bear country. Black bears aren't as big as grizzlies. They stand about six feet or so, and they don't have the bad reputation grizzlies have. But I was on foot and close to them. That was scary. Black bears are very strong and have sharp teeth and claws.

I walked along adrift in the heat and humming insects. Another bear sighting. This time I saw a yearling cinnamon bear, a reddish color version of the black bear. I yelled and clapped my hands. The sound startled both of us. It fled.

I continued walking, the only sound, the creaking of my backpack. The humming of insects lulled me into a trancelike state. Three hours passed. I looked down the narrow trail and saw open sunlight. It was the meadow I had to cross to reach the river where Orville would pick me up. I quickened my step, anxious to be rid of my heavy pack.

Suddenly sharp scraping sounds and a loud *whoosh* came from the forest twenty feet away. I froze. Looking toward the source of the noise, I saw two black bear cubs shinny up a tree as fast as they could. *Oh no*, I thought, *not again.*

Yikes!
Here comes Mama!

Then Mama Bear rose up on her hind legs, taller than me. She dropped down and charged. I remembered the sign I had seen in Alaska.

```
WHAT TO DO IN CASE OF BEAR ATTACK
DROP THE PACK AND SLOWLY BACK AWAY
WATCH THE BEAR ALL THE WHILE
CALMLY TALK TO IT
```

I dropped the pack, turned, and without a word, ran as fast as I could for a hundred yards.

I stopped, turned, and gasped for breath, panting with fear. The bear was rolling all over the ground with my pack.

I yelled and clapped my hands. The bear wasn't buying it. She had cubs to protect.

She charged again. I ran again. This time, I kept going, finally rounding a bend in the trail.

I stopped and waited, prepared to run again. I couldn't see beyond the bend. Was she coming after me?

In the distance I heard an outboard motor. It got louder, then stopped. Orville! The bear was between Orville and me. I waited, trying to catch my breath. Five minutes—ten minutes. The motor started up again and then faded off in the distance. Silence. Orville was gone. I waited. No bear. The only way to the river was by this trail, so I slowly retraced my steps, reached the bend, and peeked around. No bear.

I started singing as loudly as I could to warn her that I was coming. It sounded awful. I can't sing at all. I hoped the bear felt the same way. I found my pack. She had chewed up the sleeping pad, and not feeling threatened anymore, rounded up her cubs and left.

I slipped on the pack and crossed the bright meadow to the river. I dropped the pack and slid down the steep, sandy bank, waded neck deep into the wide, brown Peace River, and waited for Orville to return.

Orville, what took you so long?

# AUTHOR'S NOTE

Black bears are found throughout Alaska and Canada, in the mountains of the western United States, and in the eastern United States as far south as Louisiana and Florida. Their coats range from glossy black to dark brown, reddish brown, or almost white. Adult bears can reach a height of six feet when standing on their hind legs. Black bears will eat just about anything: fruit, nuts, roots, honey, insects, rodents, fish, carrion, and even garbage. Their sense of smell is much better than their sense of sight or hearing. They sleep during the coldest part of winter, living off their stored fat.

Wood Buffalo National Park straddles the border between Alberta and the Northwest Territories in Canada. Larger than Switzerland, it is one of the biggest national parks in the world. Enormous rivers flow through its subarctic wilderness of bogs, forests, lakes, and meadows. It is home to hundreds of thousands of ducks, geese, and other waterfowl. It is the only nesting site in the world of the rare whooping crane. The northernmost colony of white pelicans in North America nests on islands in the Slave River rapids. There are also wolves, moose, woodland caribou, foxes, lynx, black bears, eagles, muskrats, beavers, and wood bison.

In Sweetgrass Station several old log buildings were used to house the crews that vaccinated the bison. There is even an old slaughterhouse where bison meat was processed.

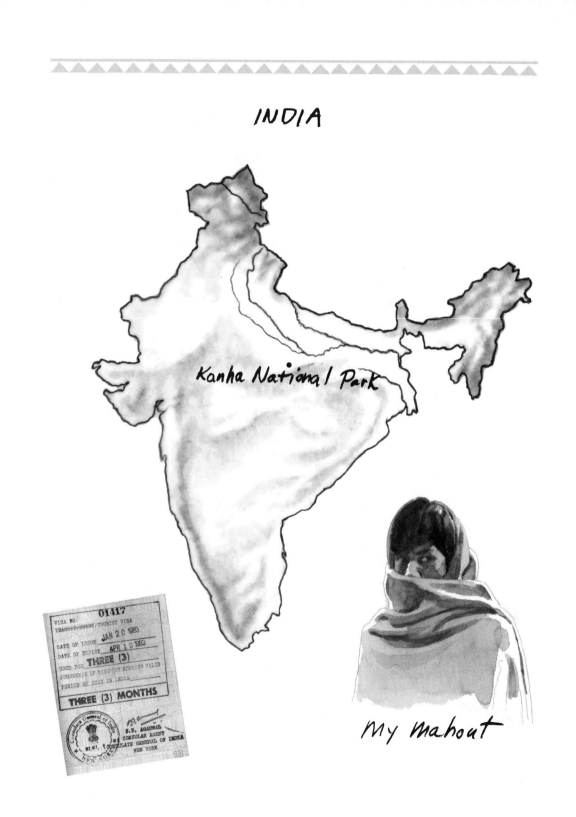

INDIA

Kanha National Park

VISA NO. **01417**
TRANSIT/ENTRY/TOURIST VISA
DATE OF ISSUE JAN 2 0 1983
DATE OF EXPIRY APR 1 9 1983
GOOD FOR **THREE (3)**
JOURNEY/S IF PASSPORT REMAINS VALID
PERIOD OF STAY IN INDIA
**THREE (3) MONTHS**
S.E. AGARWAL
CONSULAR AGENT
CONSULATE GENERAL OF INDIA
NEW YORK

My mahout

# 6/ Roar

My rondavel was just outside the entrance to Kanha National Park in central India. I had been resting inside during the hot part of the day, hoping for news about the animal I had traveled twelve thousand miles to see. An Indian man came to the door.

"We have a located tiger, sir. Do you wish to see it?" he asked.

I grabbed my camera bag, ran outside, and jumped into the waiting Jeep.

As we drove into the jungle, the driver told me that an elephant patrol had located the tiger and radioed the news to park headquarters. Forty-five minutes later we left the Jeep and began to walk on a trail through the jungle. Soon, we came upon a clearing where an elephant was waiting. Its mahout sat astride its neck.

I climbed a ladder up to the howdah, the wooden platform on the elephant's back. I was sitting fourteen feet above the ground with my legs hanging over the side of the howdah, secured by a wooden railing. We started off, the howdah rocking gently from side to side as the elephant walked. At first I held tightly to the railing, afraid of falling off, but I soon relaxed and enjoyed the motion of the ten-thousand-pound creature beneath me.

The elephant shambled across the Kanha meadow. The late afternoon sun cast long shadows from the distant kapok trees onto the meadow grass.

The mahout urged the elephant on with gentle kicks behind its ears. He talked to it constantly. Chital deer were feeding all around us. Where the final sun played full on their gorgeous coats, white spots danced.

We entered the jungle. The elephant trod a very narrow path, one foot in front of the other. The mahout stopped the elephant. We stood silently. The mahout lit a *bidi*, a dark, spicy cigarette. Its hot red tip glowed in the blue-green gloom of the jungle. He blew a cloud of thick, pungent smoke.

We waited. The elephant's stomach rumbled. Huge strangler vines entangled the trees, making an even darker chamber inside the dark jungle. By the cock of his head, the mahout seemed to be listening. He urged the elephant forward. It sighed. We began rocking gently again as if struck by the wake of a passing ship. The huge beast made no sound as it walked. We stopped again and the mahout pointed.

Just ahead lay the sleeping tiger. She was in a patch of dappled sunlight, under a *sal* tree. The tree's leaves had turned orange and littered the ground. I couldn't make her out. The

*Sleeping Beauty*

mahout kept pointing. I looked harder and the tiger materialized. Her color and stripes and the dappled light made her almost invisible. She was a Bengal tiger, one of the rarest animals on earth. No one is sure how many remain in the wild.

The mahout urged the elephant forward. It groaned in protest. Elephants and tigers avoid each other naturally in the wild.

We waited, scarcely breathing. The tigress lifted her enormous head, and her yellow eyes looked right through the elephant to the meadow beyond. She was beautiful, seven feet from her nose to the end of her long tail, now flicking. She weighed nearly three hundred pounds, twice as much as me. The mahout moved the elephant closer still.

I tapped him on the shoulder and pointed at my long lens to tell

Back off!

him we were close enough. He nod-
ded and, misunderstanding, moved
even closer. We were now fifteen feet
from the tigress, a distance she
could cover in one bound. She
was rigid and alert. I focused
my camera on her. She
filled the frame.

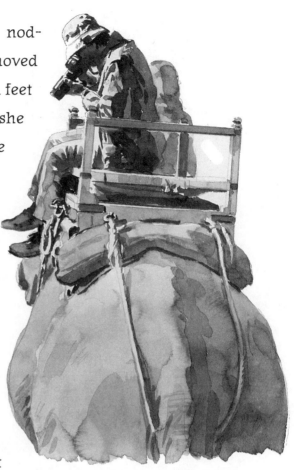

Suddenly she sprang to
her feet and roared an
intense, violent roar, not
heard so much as felt in the
guts. I jerked back instinctively and the camera shut-
ter went off. The mahout
moved the terrified elephant
back, much to my relief, not to mention the elephant's. Once we
had retreated beyond her fight-or-flight distance, the invisible
line that causes a wild animal to either attack or flee, she lay
down again, groomed, and promptly fell back asleep.

The photo I took looks like the last thing a photographer sees
before he dies.

I have heard a story of a tiger and an elephant in exactly this situation. The tiger clawed its way up the trunk of the elephant to get to the mahout. In this instance the tiger leaped away, and the elephant and its mahout were unhurt.

The Bengal tiger was once found over most of the Indian subcontinent. Bengal tigers live in dry and moist deciduous forests, bamboo forests, rain forests, evergreen forests, grasslands, and mangrove swamps, and at altitudes as high as thirteen thousand feet. A large male tiger may weigh more than four hundred pounds, a female more than three hundred pounds. The tiger's striped coat is excellent camouflage in the dappled light of the forest. Tigers silently stalk their prey and kill with a single bite to the throat or back of the neck. They are only successful in one out of ten hunts. Unlike other cats, tigers love water. After a 105-day gestation period, cubs are born blind and helpless. They spend about twenty months with their mother.

Approximately 1.2 billion people, or 20 percent of the world's population, share land with the tiger, which puts great pressure on its habitat. The fragmentation of a habitat and dam building, along with poaching for organs, bones, fur, and claws, have made the Bengal tiger an extremely endangered animal. There are perhaps only a few thousand Bengal tigers left in the wild. The people of India have always venerated the tiger in religion and folklore.

UGANDA

Kibale Forest
National Park

Before the hunt

# 7 / The Meat Eaters of Kibale

In the forest it was pitch-black and raining. The headlights went out again. This was the fourth time they had failed. David, my driver, got out, poked around, and the lights came back on. They shot a narrow tunnel of light through the rain. I could just make out the shapes of big trees and tangled vines on the sides of the road. We were on our way to Kibale Forest National Park in southwestern Uganda, home to some of the last wild chimps left in Uganda, or anywhere else in Africa.

We arrived at the park headquarters at first light. It was a small stucco building. One entire outside wall was painted with life-size portraits of chimps against a bright blue background. From this vantage point I looked out over the top of the rain forest. Through my binoculars I could see a troop of red colobus monkeys feeding in the topmost branches of a huge fig tree.

I was introduced to Godfrey, who would guide me to the chimps. He was a small Ugandan man dressed in a neat olive green uniform. He said we should hurry because the chimps were moving quickly through the trees. Soon they would be too far away for us to follow on foot.

I followed Godfrey onto a trail just behind park headquarters. We heard the whoops and screams of the chimps echoing through the forest as we picked our way along a narrow elephant trail. We passed big pools deep in the forest created by elephants wallowing, and caught glimpses of monkeys in the highest branches. The chimp screams grew louder. Then there were even louder whoops and barks and wails. They sounded like children throwing tantrums and screaming at the top of their lungs.

We passed under a towering *monodura* tree. Suddenly the big

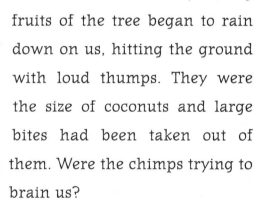

fruits of the tree began to rain down on us, hitting the ground with loud thumps. They were the size of coconuts and large bites had been taken out of them. Were the chimps trying to brain us?

Up ahead we saw a chimp drop down through the branches and vines to the ground. He ran along, upright on his feet. Others joined him. We followed.

BA BOOM! BA BOOM! BA BOOM!

Then we heard the sound of loud hollow drumming. Through the dense cover, I could just make out a big male chimp beating on the wide buttress of a fig tree trunk with his open hands. Then he swung up into the trees and disappeared. All the screaming and whooping stopped. We waited. A few minutes later we heard them again. But now they seemed to be miles away.

The next day we went back to the forest. We carefully skirted a line of safari ants, making sure not to pick up any on our clothing. Their bite is like the sting of a wasp. Godfrey's radio crackled. He talked into it, listened, then smiled. We immediately changed direction and bushwhacked through the tangled undergrowth. After last night's rain it was slippery underfoot.

We came upon a young woman and two men with notebooks.

They were looking up into the forest canopy. They had been following and studying this troop of chimps for days. I looked where they were looking. I saw a big female chimp 150 feet up in the top of a *munusops* tree. She held what was left of a red colobus monkey—shredded fur, bloodred meat, and the head, smashed and broken—in her lap.

The researchers told me what had happened. The chimp community had gathered to feast on the ripening munusops fruit. Then they spotted a troop of red colobus monkeys. By working together the chimps would greatly increase their chances of catching the monkeys.

 The male chimps organized the hunt as if they were generals in a campaign. First they chased the terrified red colobus troop through the treetops. The female chimps stayed on the ground, screaming madly to confuse the monkeys. The colobus males turned back and confronted the chimps to allow their females and young to flee. They put up a fierce fight with chimps that were many times their size. Finally trapped, they were overwhelmed and killed.

It fell to the dominant male chimp to divide up the meat

according to rules only he understood. Some chimps received a share. Others didn't. I knew that it was a recent discovery that chimps would eat meat and even hunt for it. I could hardly believe I was actually seeing the results of such a hunt.

Now the big female sat with her share of the spoils. She daintily picked at long shreds of fur-covered flesh with her fingertips. A chorus of great whoops and barks and ear-shattering screams echoed through the dripping forest as the chimps squabbled and called to one another. The female rose with the remains of the monkey dangling from her mouth. She knuckle-walked across a branch bridge to the next tree. She moved easily through the tree highway and found a suitable branch to lean back on, one hand behind her head. She reached out languidly, plucking ripe munusops fruit, as if they were after-dinner mints.

## AUTHOR'S NOTE

**Hot and tired**

Chimps live in troops containing 10 or sometimes more than 100 animals. They have a well-defined territory that is fiercely defended by regular patrols. Chimps are primarily fruit eaters, but, occasionally, they eat meat. Most kills are opportunistic, but stalking prey is not unusual.

Chimps are among the most intelligent animals. They will use stems or twigs as tools to extract ants and termites from their holes. They are more closely related to humans than any other living creature. Chimps can stand 5½ feet tall and weigh 175 pounds, the size of an average man. They have an arm span of 7 feet and are stronger than any man. They can live to be forty years old.

Kibale Forest National Park, in southwest Uganda, opened in 1993. It is 1,233 square miles, four times the size of New York City. A rain forest with patches of swamp and grassland, the park has the greatest concentration of primates anywhere in East Africa. Its 13 species include red colobus, black-and-white colobus, vervet monkeys, blue monkeys, olive baboons, and chimpanzees. Kibale is also home to lions, leopards, forest elephants, buffalo, hippos, forest hogs, and 335 bird species, including the Prigogines ground thrush, which is found only in Uganda.

Due to overpopulation and war, the world of the chimps is vanishing. In some places, they are hunted for food.

Home of the chimps

# MANITOBA, CANADA

Churchill
Polar bear
capital

CUSTOMS
IMMIGRATION
DOUANES
IMMIGRATION
9 VII 1984
TORONTO
248

# 8 / Barnstorming

I was standing on the dock of the floatplane base, waiting for Doug, my pilot. I had come up to Churchill in northern Manitoba, Canada, on the overnight sleeper from Winnipeg, known as the Muskeg Special. It was the only rail line into and out of town. I was hoping to see some of the polar bears that were gathered here at the edge of Hudson Bay. They were waiting for the bay to freeze so they could hunt seals on the ice. I had seen one big polar bear so far, down by the garbage dump. Not really what I had in mind.

Doug swaggered down the dock, sporting a cracked leather jacket and a white scarf around his neck, thrown over one shoulder like a barnstormer. He shook my hand, then climbed up on

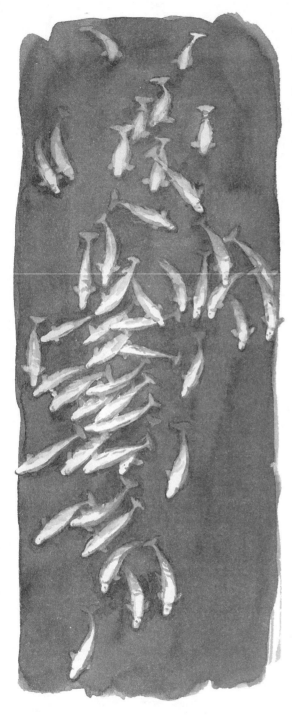

the wing and added extra fuel to the old red-and-white floatplane. I stuffed myself into the seat next to his and buckled up. Doug slid in beside me, flashed a Hollywood grin, and started the engine.

The plane coughed to life. The propeller jerked a couple of times, then started to spin. Doug put on his headset, motioning for me to do the same. I saw his mouth making words, but all I heard was the roar of the engine. Doug swung the plane away from the dock, put her into the wind, and gunned the engine. We lurched forward and began to bump on the chop of the water. The plane tilted back so far that I couldn't see anything over the dashboard. The bumping quickened, then suddenly stopped as we lifted off, climbed, and banked steeply to the left. My stomach went into my throat.

The ground dropped away sharply and the horizon tipped one way, then the other. It made me very dizzy. I saw the big grain elevator and the old wrecked ship in the harbor. They looked like toys now.

Mama and calf

We flew east along the coast and saw endless rocky points jutting far out into the bay. We spotted six polar bears, all dazzling white against the tundra. Doug opened the window. Freezing air rushed in. Then he banked the plane at a right angle. I almost threw up.

We turned back toward Churchill. Doug banked the plane again and my knees got weak. He pointed down. It was the Churchill River, wide and black, jam-packed with beluga whales and their young. The whales' white bodies looked blue-green in the water. There were hundreds of them.

I gave Doug a thumbs-up. He smiled and we banked sharply again. The horizon tipped so far, I held onto my seat for dear life and closed my eyes. Then Doug banked the plane in the other direction. My stomach went back up into my throat. I swallowed hard. As he leveled the plane, I looked down. The sun glinted off a patchwork of ponds. Thousands of pure white snow geese flew below us.

I looked past Doug through the open window and saw the shoreline of Hudson Bay. On a small, rocky island stood a polar bear. The bear, hearing the plane, loped into the water. It came up to his shoulders. He stood up on his hind legs and watched us roar over.

"Should we have another go at that?" Doug shouted. I nod-ded, afraid that if I opened my mouth, I'd lose my lunch. We circled back for another look. Now the bear was swimming, his big paws splayed out in the water. He rolled over on his back and watched us disappear into the lowering sun. I thought of him swimming alone in the enormous silence of Hudson Bay, the only sounds his breathing and the soft splashing of his paws.

The base came into view. We landed, and glided up to the dock. Doug cut the motor and the prop sputtered to a stop. I climbed out,

*I'm outta here!*

half frozen, weak-kneed, and a little green.

"So, how was that?" Doug asked, grinning as he threw his scarf over his shoulder.

"Cool!" I answered. As he walked down the dock, I yelled, "You don't have any openings tomorrow, do you?"

## AUTHOR'S NOTE

*Polar bears range across the Arctic. They are the largest land carnivores in the world, followed in size by coastal grizzlies and Siberian tigers. Unlike other bears, polar bears are mainly carnivorous. Their primary source of food is ringed and bearded seals. They eat walrus and beluga* whales to a lesser extent. They will also eat carrion and garbage. Any living creatures they encounter, including humans, are potential prey. They have a good sense of smell and hearing, and they see as well as humans.

Polar bears have a creamy white coat that camouflages them in the ice and snow. They have been observed covering their black noses with their white paws while hunting seals. The fur between their toes helps them maintain footholds on the ice. They are huge, reaching a height of more than eight feet when standing on their hind feet, and weigh more than 1,500 pounds. Even a 150-pound cub is stronger than any man.

Normally solitary, polar bears congregate in large numbers near Churchill in the fall. The bears that come too close to town and could

pose a danger to humans are trapped and housed in a building called a bear jail until Hudson Bay freezes over. Then they are tranquilized and taken by helicopter out onto the sea ice and set free.

Since the last glacier retreated eight thousand years ago, the land around Churchill has been springing back from the release of this great weight, rising at about three feet per year. The advance and retreat of the glaciers and the resulting gravel ridges interspersed with fens and bogs are typical of the *tundra along Hudson Bay. There is high boreal forest, subarctic forest of spruce, lichen park lands, and treeless tundra. The area is dominated by muskeg, a swamp formed by accumulations of sphagnum moss and decaying leaves. There is permafrost a foot or so beneath the sphagnum moss, gravel, and ponds.*

*The tundra along Hudson Bay is an incredible patchwork of arctic flora: dwarf birch and willows, avens, mosses, crowberry, alder thickets, cloudberry, arctic dewberry, and blackberry. Besides polar bears and belugas, snow geese, sandhill cranes, willow ptarmigan, Pacific loons, ravens, arctic and red foxes, black bears, caribous, thousands of shorebirds, ducks, and songbirds make this fragile land their home.*

# ALBERTA, CANADA

Wood Buffalo
National Park

CUSTOMS
IMMIGRATION
DOUANES
IMMIGRATION
9 VII 1984
TORONTO
248

cross fox

In a hurry!

# 9/Sleeping with Bison

My Cree Indian guide, George Martin, shut the motor and paddled the red aluminum skiff silently up to the rocky shore. That morning we left from his little village, Fort Chipewyan in Alberta, Canada. We had followed the north shore of Lake Claire. Heading into Wood Buffalo National Park, we passed Indians smoking salmon on wooden racks, beavers, bald eagles, and a massive old bull bison that was swimming across the lake. We got so close to him that we could see his bloodshot eyes.

"There's a big herd where we're going," George told me.

We stepped out of the boat, ducked low, and lay down behind a fallen snag. I peeked over the snag and then looked at George. He turned and smiled at me. In front of us, just as he promised, was a herd of three hundred wood bison, bigger, blacker, and shaggier than their plains brothers, every one about the size of a minivan.

Taking a dust bath

We watched the bison as they grazed, grunted, snorted, and chewed their cuds. One huge fellow rubbed his bearded chin and face on a low rise. Finally he fell over on his back, sending up a big dust cloud as he bathed in the dry dirt. We were very close, twenty-five yards and downwind, so they couldn't smell us.

George whispered, "The minute we stand, they will stampede."

HOLY COW!

We stood up. Off they went, shaking the ground like an earthquake.

As we set up camp, I noticed that the herd had stopped at the other end of the meadow, about a half mile away.

At five o'clock the next morning I awoke in my tent to the sounds of groaning, grunting, and snorting close by. Still lying in my sleeping bag, I slowly unzipped the tent flap and pulled it back. Outside the triangle of the tent opening I saw a forest of legs and hooves. Huge, shaggy bodies surrounded me.

My little tent was in the middle of the bison herd. Through the forest of legs I could see the horizon, a cutout of stunted spruce trees against an orange streak where the sun was rising. Smaller legs and hooves of the red-golden calves moved in the midst of the larger black legs of the adults. It had rained over-

night, and the bison were churning the area around my tent into thick black muck that sucked at their hooves. Long strands of drool hung from their noses and mouths, sparkling in the sun.

The deep grunts and snorts all around me were oddly reassuring. I could make out shaggy shadow shapes through the translucent tent. Separated only by thin nylon, I knew exactly how it felt to be part of the herd, safe and secure in their numbers—peaceful. It never entered my mind that the bison might stampede and trample my tent. Big steaming buffalo chips fell outside my tent door, as if they had dropped from the sky. The forest of legs and hooves was so thick, I could no longer see the horizon.

Suddenly the ground trembled beneath me. The bison disappeared. The forest had been clear-cut in an instant.

A lone white wolf stood at the edge of the spruce forest.

## AUTHOR'S NOTE

*In 1893 there were only five hundred wood bison remaining in Canada. Wood Buffalo National Park was established in 1922 to protect the last remaining herd of wood bison. Soon after the park was created, sixty-six hundred plains bison were moved by rail and river barge from Alberta. The two species intermingled, and now all the bison in the park* may be hybrids. This herd is the largest free-roaming herd of wood bison in the world.

Wood bison can attain a height of at least six feet and a length of almost twelve feet, which includes a one-and-a-half-foot tail. Wolves are their only predator. Attacking in packs, wolves can take on an older, injured bison by worrying it over several days until it is weak enough for an easy kill.

Fort Chipewyan, established in 1788, is the oldest continuously inhabited settlement in Alberta. No paved roads lead to it. On its short main street, there is a nice little café that serves a delicious breakfast.

# NEW YORK, U.S.

Harriman
State Park

## Lake Skenonto

Just a bus ride away from N.Y.C.

# 10 / Rattler

mushroom

"Where's *he* going?" said the woman.

"Africa?" her friend answered with a snicker.

We were standing in the Port Authority bus terminal in New York City. I was wearing khaki shorts and shirt, hiking boots, and a backpack with a sleeping bag strapped to the bottom. Everyone else was dressed for work: shirts, ties, business suits.

I wasn't going to Africa. I was going upstate to Harriman State Park in the Ramapo Mountains just thirty miles from New York City. I love its rugged, rocky hiking, its sheer cliffs, and its lakes, wildflowers, mushrooms, deer, and caves used by horse thieves during the Revolutionary War—a paradise left to the people of New York by the railroad magnate E. H. Harriman.

I got off the bus in Tuxedo, New York, and found the trailhead behind the old railroad station. My favorite part of this hike was climbing the steep, rocky trail up into the woods. With each step, the roar of the cars and trucks on the nearby thruway lessened.

Eventually I heard only the sound of birdsong and the rustling of leaves in the trees. I followed the yellow trail blazes painted on the trees. My destination was Lake Skenonto, the

Indian name for "place of the deer," a beautiful, lily-covered lake with a tiny, rocky islet and its own little forest in the middle. I planned to camp there for two nights. I hoped to see the white deer that had been sighted there.

The trail through the woods became an old fire road now overgrown with tall grass. The sun glinted through the trees, and scarlet tanagers flitted about in the highest branches. Suddenly I heard a sound that stopped me dead in my tracks, a sound I'd never heard before, but instinctively knew. It was a buzzing rattle unlike anything else. I froze and looked all around me.

There it was, fifteen feet away, coiled in a patch of sunlight in

the middle of the road. A timber rattlesnake, a highly venomous snake. Its tail vibrated so quickly, it looked blurred. The rattle it made was terrifying.

I watched it, transfixed. The sound of the rattle never let up. I took a step back. The sound softened. Two steps back, softer yet.

I waited. The rattling stopped. I watched as the snake uncoiled and slid through the grass, into the forest. It was almost six feet long. I thought, *What a wild thing to see only thirty miles from New York City!*

What a beauty!

That night as I unrolled my sleeping bag beside the lake, I remembered a photo I'd seen in a newspaper a while back. It showed a smiling New York City police officer holding up a six-foot-long rattlesnake by the tail. He had shot it in some terrified citizen's backyard in Brooklyn.

The next morning I was sitting quietly by the shore. I sensed a presence and looked up. A few feet away I saw a white deer, drinking from the lake. I made a slight movement that startled her. She snorted and bolted into the woods.

# AUTHOR'S NOTE

The timber rattlesnake is the only rattler found in northeastern United States. Timber rattlers are pit vipers. The sensory pits on each side of their heads detect heat given off by their warm-blooded prey. The rattle is a series of flattened hollow segments that make a noise when the rattle is shaken. Each of these segments was once the tip of the rattler's tail. A new one is added each time the snake sheds its skin.

Timber rattlers do a lot of preliminary rattling before striking. They congregate in large numbers to bask and hibernate on rocky cliffs, a habit that has made it easy for humans to catch or kill them. This makes them popular with snake-handling religious cults in the mountains in the southern states. There have been many fatalities from snakebites among these snake handlers.

Bear Mountain-Harriman State Park was established in 1910 through a gift of money and ten thousand acres of land from Mary Williamson Harriman. The park is now forty thousand acres of glaciated hills and valleys, twenty-two lakes, and many miles of hiking trails, including a section of the Appalachian Trail. In the area a number of Revolutionary War battles were fought, and there were once many Indian villages and campsites.

How many rattlers can you find in this picture?

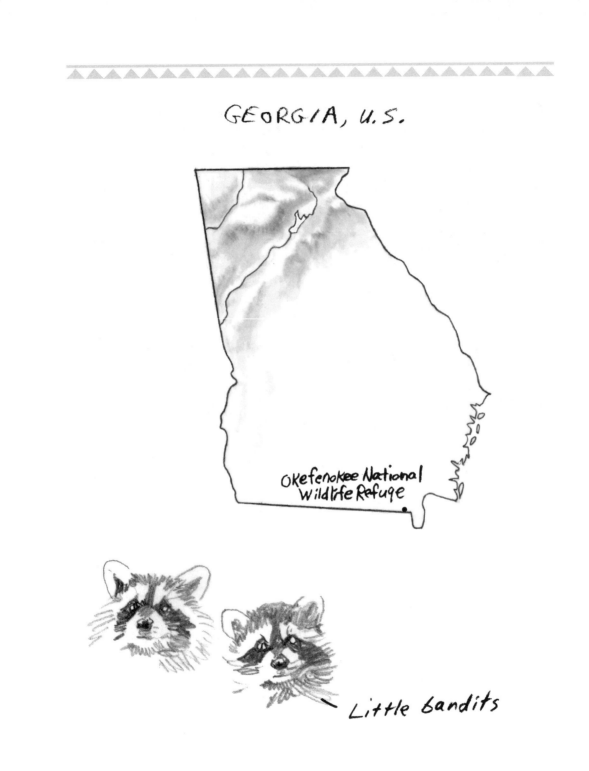

GEORGIA, U.S.

Okefenokee National
Wildlife Refuge

Little bandits

# 11 / Deputy Dawg

*ya hoo!*

I shivered as I broke the skim ice around the canoe with my paddle and pushed off from the wooden platform into the open water. It was the coldest winter in the Okefenokee Swamp in years. The temperature was below freezing, and I wasn't prepared for it. I didn't have enough warm clothes and my feet felt like blocks of ice.

I knew it was unlikely that I'd see alligators or snakes. You wouldn't expect to see those cold-blooded animals in such cold weather. But the flocks of sandhill cranes, beautiful long-necked, long-legged birds with a red splash of color on their heads, made up for it and the cold.

*Brrrr!*

Sniff
Sniff

I was doing a week-long, fifty-mile trip in the swamp. I needed to make it to the next wooden sleeping platform before dark each day.

There was no dry ground for camping in the swamp, except for John's Island, my next stop. John's Island had a small cabin. It also had a bear. I had been told to be careful.

Hours later, I drifted up onto a much-used landing spot on John's Island. The minute I touched dry land, a big mother raccoon, the size of a *very* big house cat, and two half-grown cubs jumped into the bow of my canoe. *Funny,* I thought, *Raccoons are nocturnal animals.*

The raccoons tore at my backpack with their handlike paws, looking for food. I poked them with the paddle but couldn't dissuade them, so I grabbed my backpack and pulled. The raccoons tugged at the other end with their teeth. We carried on like this for a few more minutes. Finally I dragged my backpack off the canoe. The raccoons were still attached.

Once on land they relented but stayed hot on my heels as I headed up the path to my cabin. I passed the sign-in box and read the comments left by the last campers. In large script it read: *Beware of Deputy Dawg!*

I looked down at the raccoons. One cub came forward and stood on its hind legs. I leaned over to take his picture. He grabbed the camera and swung on it. Meanwhile, his mother was tearing at the backpack again.

I finally put all my gear into the cabin, but there was no way to lock the door, so I wedged the frame of my backpack under the doorknob. I looked out the window. Mama stationed herself outside the cabin door. The cubs were play-wrestling.

I had encountered raccoons many times before. One night in the Florida Everglades about ten of them surrounded the tent next to mine, looking for food. It scared the first-time campers half to death.

"What are they?" "What do they want?" I heard them whisper to one another. I knew the raccoons weren't dangerous, but wild animals with no fear of humans can still be disconcerting.

I opened a can of sardines for supper and went back outside. I sat down on the cabin steps. Three masked faces stared at me. I ignored them. Mama bit the toe of my boot, hard. *This is not going to work*, I thought.

I went into the cabin again. I sat with my back against the door to keep it closed, and finished my supper while Mama scratched at the door. I unrolled my sleeping bag against the door and got into it. The raccoons climbed up on the wire mesh windows and shook them. Next I heard paws on the roof. Dust and grime fell down the chimney into the fireplace.

It continued this way all night, nonstop. The raccoons threw themselves against the door, shook the windows, and scampered across the roof over and over again.

*Where's the bear?* I thought. *Gimme the bear* any *day.*

FEED ME! I'M HUNGRY!

# AUTHOR'S NOTE

*Raccoons are curious, adaptable animals. They usually live in woods and swamps near water, but can even be found in cities, scavenging for food. They have a "bandit" mask across their eyes and a bushy tail ringed with black bands. Their front paws have long, sensitive toes, which they use like fingers. They eat rodents, birds, turtle eggs, nuts, seeds, fruit, frogs, and fish. The way they scoop frogs or fish out of the water probably gave rise to the myth that they wash their food. Their footprints look almost human. I've seen them in the snow in my backyard in Brooklyn.*

*The Indian name Okefenokee means "trembling earth." It refers to the floating peat islands in the swamp that rise and fall underfoot.*

*The Okefenokee stretches over southeast Georgia, encompassing an area that is twice the size of New York City. It gives birth to the St. Mary's and Suwannee Rivers. It is home to two hundred species of birds, forty species of mammals, more than fifty species of reptiles, and thirty-two species of amphibians, along with thirty-four different kinds of fish. It contains islands, lakes, clusters of trees and underbrush called hammocks, open expanses of grass and aquatic plants called prairies, majestic cypress trees, and insect-eating plants.*

*The tannic acid from decaying vegetation makes the water the color of strong tea. Because the water is so dark, it reflects like a mirror, so it is hard to tell the real sky and trees from the ones in the water.*

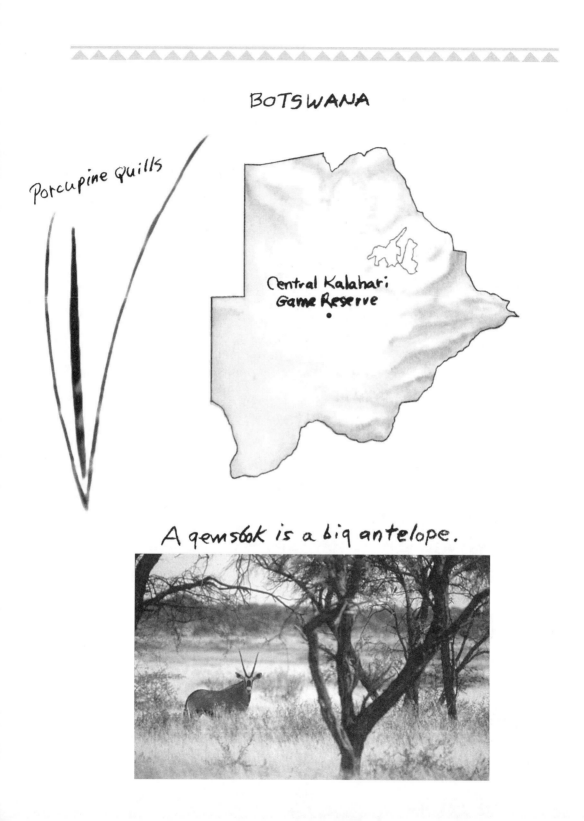

BOTSWANA

Porcupine Quills

Central Kalahari
Game Reserve

A gemsbok is a big antelope.

# 12 / Downwind of a Dung Beetle

Here he comes like a steamroller. Nothing can stop him. The dung beetle pushes his prize before him in the soft sand over dunes and into gullies with amazing speed and agility. I decide to see what it looks like from the dung beetle's point of view.

I lie down, flat on the sand of the Kalahari desert. The dung beetle crashes along, pushing the dung ball that is ten times his size with his pronged back legs. He falls into holes, tumbles over, and back up again. I can see why dung beetles are sometimes called tumblebugs. His back legs embrace the dung ball, rolling it ever onward.

My dung beetle can't see where he's going, only where he's been. Then I wonder how well dung beetles can see. I know they sure smell. I've never watched one before. I'm fascinated.

I move along with my dung beetle. I have to scurry on my belly to keep up. I'm so close I can hear the scraping and crashing

as he blunders through the tall grass. From his perspective, the grass looks like a miniature forest. Humps in the sand look like miniature mountains. The wind shifts and is now blowing from him to me. Definitely not the best situation for dung beetle watching.

My dung beetle and I have covered about forty feet together, he on his dung ball and me on my belly. Dung beetles have been clocked moving at 754 feet, or more than the length of two football fields, per hour.

My dung beetle rolls the ball out onto a clear sandy patch and into a shallow gully. He tumbles in after it. He rolls it up the other side of the gully to a narrow hole in the sand, into which he disappears, leaving his dung ball behind.

I'm slowly baking in the blazing sun, looking at a ball of dung, waiting for something to happen. I wonder, *Whose dung is it*? It could be from a hartebeest, a wildebeest, a gemsbok, a lion, or . . . *no*, it couldn't be. I buried mine.

The wind is steady on, blowing right over the dung and into my nostrils. Nothing happens. The naked dung just sits there.

*All done!*

What if there were no dung beetles? Who would clean up after those huge herds of wildebeests, kudus, hartebeests, elands, and gemsboks, not to mention lions, leopards, warthogs, brown hyenas, mongooses, and bat-eared foxes out there in the Kalahari? Dung beetles can clean up one thousand pounds of dung per acre each year. They have been around for such a long time that they even cleaned up after the dinosaurs.

It's so hot that I'm about to abandon my project when I see a surge of sand spill out of the hole and cascade down the side of the gully. The beetle appears in the opening and surveys the situation. He goes back inside, then out again, pushing a wall of sand before him with his shovel-shaped, dung-covered nose. He repeats this procedure over and over again.

I can see that when he enters the chamber, he makes a sharp turn. This is where he's excavating the sand. When it's ready, he scurries out of the hole and down to his beloved ball of dung. He mounts it. Up the incline he goes. He loses the ball. It rolls back down.

On the second attempt, he rolls the ball into the hole and his chamber. I can see him patting his dung ball tenderly, touching it all over with all six legs. Finally he rolls it into the newly renovated quarters.

A few moments later he comes back out, squatting thoughtfully in dung-covered splendor at his entrance hole. Inside, his hard-won prize awaits his leisure.

I get up, brush off the sand, and decide to go see if *mine* is still safe and sound where I buried it.

## AUTHOR'S NOTE

egg
in brood ball

larva

pupa

There are four thousand species of dung beetle worldwide. Seven hundred and eighty species are found in southern Africa.

The dung beetle lays an egg on the dung ball. The egg changes to a larva that feeds on the dung, then into a pupa. Eventually an adult beetle emerges from the hole and flies away.

The ancient Egyptians noted that a beetle would bury a dung ball and a beetle would emerge from the hole one month later. They thought it was the same beetle. To the Egyptians, the beetle's behavior represented the rebirth of the sun and the promise of new life. The beetle was their sacred scarab symbolizing their sun god, Ra. They worshiped it as the power that propelled the sun across the sky.

Dung beetles are amazingly strong. They can roll a ball of dung up to forty times their own mass. It is believed that they use the sun to guide them in a straight line.

By removing dung these beetles help control the population of fly species and the spread of disease. They help improve the soil and spread natural fertilizers. They carefully pick seeds out of the dung and leave them on the surface of the soil, where they have a better chance of germinating.

Large dung beetles are extremely difficult to hold in a clenched fist. They can live for four years and, not surprisingly, have an exceptional sense of smell.

Jade scarabs
from Cairo.
Actual size.

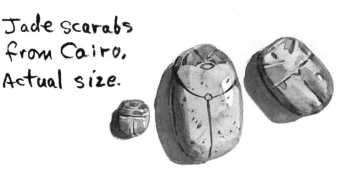

FLORIDA, U.S.

Key Largo

Hawksbill turtle
taking a breather
at the surface.

# 13 / The Joker

Captain Bell sat up on the flying bridge as he maneuvered the dive boat out of the marina at Key Largo. We were heading for Molasses Reef in the Florida Keys, a string of islands off the southern tip of Florida. The boat was packed with scuba divers all gearing up as we hit open water. I had only a mask, snorkel, and flippers. I loved snorkeling the clear, shallow waters that teemed with endless varieties of colorful fish, moray eels, manta rays, and turtles.

When we arrived at the dive site, parts of the reef were exposed with low tide. The water was calm and clear. A cabin cruiser was anchored nearby. People sunbathed on the deck. Just as the divers helped one another put on their tanks and checked their regulators, we heard someone yell, "SHARK! SHARK!" It sounded burbled. The person was swimming frantically. His mouth was half full of water. The people on the cabin cruiser laughed at his attempt to scare the divers on our boat.

We had just been about to go into the water. We glanced at one another, wide-eyed behind our masks. In all the years I'd been diving, I'd never seen a shark in the water. I looked at the captain. He was disgusted by the joker's attempt to scare off his clients.

Captain Bell climbed up on the bridge for a look. We heard "SHARK! *burble* SHARK! *burble*" from the water. The joker finally climbed up on his boat, quickly pulled up anchor, and left. Captain Bell said he saw nothing in the water, so the divers splashed in, feet first, holding their masks tightly to their faces. Then Captain Bell directed me to the edge of the reef where snorkeling would be best.

I jumped in, cleared my snorkel, and finned over to the reef a couple hundred yards away. When the sun-dappled reef wall appeared out of the void, the first thing I saw was an eye, a great big, round, cold staring eye. I looked harder as I lay on the surface, washing lightly back and forth with the wave action. The sun dapple obscured outlines. Starting from the eye, I looked to the left. A pointed nose and teeth—*lots* of teeth—slowly became evident. I looked to the right. More sun dapple. Then about ten feet back a sickle-shaped tail materialized. When I finally put it all together, I had one enormous, sun-dappled shark sitting stock-still, staring at me with an eye that was the size of a silver dollar. The shark-burbling joker hadn't been joking after all.

My heart jumped. Sharks rarely attack scuba divers when they're underwater. But now I was floating on the surface, like bait. I knew it was more likely that I'd be hit by lightning than that I'd be attacked by a shark but, nevertheless, I was *terrified*.

I looked for my boat. It was bobbing on the surface a hundred yards away like a bathtub toy. I began to swim backward, slowly, not taking my eyes off that single cold eye, which stared at me. The shark moved off in the opposite direction, and I lost it in the

## FACE TO FACE!

void of the deep water. I swam as fast and smoothly as I could, trying to avoid making surface sound and vibration, which would attract the shark's attention.

It was the longest swim of my life. When I climbed up the boat ladder and pulled off my mask, I was shaking like a leaf. Captain

Bell looked at me quizzically.

"Shark," I said, teeth chattering from fear.

He shook his head. "Not you, too."

Then he saw that my hands were still shaking. He climbed up on the flying bridge and scanned the reef edge with his binoculars.

"Oh, I see him now," he said. "He's a big one. A bull shark. Nothing to worry about, though. There's plenty for him to eat around here."

"Like me," I replied.

## AUTHOR'S NOTE

*A barrier reef is a long ridge of rocklike coral near a coast, separated from the mainland by a deep lagoon. Coral are fragile skeletons secreted by millions of marine polyps. Any small change in the environment can damage them. The Great Barrier Reef off the coast of Australia is the largest living thing in the world. The coral reef off the Florida Keys is the*

only barrier reef in the continental United States.

Among fish, sharks are the oldest inhabitants of the seas. They first appeared about 350 million years ago, before dinosaurs walked the earth, and they have changed little since. There are 370 species, ranging in size from six inches to forty feet. Sharks have an acute sense of smell. They can see in dim light, just like cats. A lateral line runs the length of a shark's body to help it sense its environment. Toothed sharks have multiple rows of razor-sharp teeth. When a tooth is lost, another moves forward to replace it.

Bull shark teeth... Life-size

Bull sharks grow to about eleven feet and weigh about five hundred pounds. They are the most aggressive sharks. A bull shark's lower teeth are designed to hold prey while its upper triangular teeth gouge out flesh. A bull shark will attack prey that is as large as itself.

Bull sharks can live in fresh water as well as in salt water. They regularly prowl in shallow water, making contact with humans more likely to occur. They may be territorial, and may attack if they feel cornered. There have been sixty-nine reported attacks on humans by bull sharks, seventeen of them fatal. However, dogs bite many more people than sharks do.

Humans are dangerous to sharks as well. One hundred million sharks are killed by humans each year for food and medicine, or from being tangled and drowned in fishing nets.

# UGANDA

Murchison Falls
National Park

Mama and young

# 14 / Garbage Elephants

While I was waiting for the ferry to return from the opposite bank, I knelt down to wash my hands and face in the Nile River. It had been a hot, dusty drive through the savanna of Murchison Falls National Park in Uganda. I returned to the combi (a kind of minibus). Basil, my driver, pulled us onto the ferry. I got out and stood on the deck for a better view. Hippos whooshed and grunted in the river, looking shiny pink in the late afternoon sun. I sketched some crocs as long as Cadillacs lying, mouths agape, sunbathing on a sandbar.

On a high bluff ahead of us I could see Parra Lodge, built low and solid, like an old fort. Just in front of it were two large trees laden with vultures. As we drove off the ferry and up to the lodge, a reception committee of

maribou storks waited. The storks looked like bent old men, their hands clasped behind their backs. Then we heard that elephants were at the back of the lodge, eating garbage.

"Don't get too close," the cook warned as he tossed trash into a container behind the kitchen. "Mama can be very dangerous."

I crept along the wall of the lodge and peeked around the corner, into the kitchen courtyard. There they were—the garbage elephants—one enormous cow, two young, and one tiny baby, having a fine old time with the kitchen scraps.

I could hardly believe my eyes. Elephants eating garbage! After seeing herds of these dignified giants out on the savanna throwing dust over their backs, reaching for tender leaves in the highest branches with their long trunks, pushing over young trees for forage, and splashing in ecstasy in the river, now I saw

elephants eating garbage out of big bins. I took a few pictures, then got out my sketchbook and crept to within fifty feet.

The elephants were rooting in the potato peels when Mama Elephant picked up my scent. She turned on her back legs as if on gimbals, her ears fanned out, her trunk raised like a periscope. I backed up quickly, turned the corner, and plastered myself against the wall.

The elephants roared out of the alleyway, trumpeting all the while. They formed a circus parade down the road. Despite the close encounter, I couldn't help laughing. When the elephants got a safe distance away, Baby turned and faced me. He shook his head from side to side, ran in circles, stood up on his hind legs, tried to stand on his head, and finally fell over, exhausted. Little puffs of dust blew up from his trunk with every breath. Mama came back, herded him along, and they disappeared in their own dust.

That night *Viva Las Vegas*, a movie starring Elvis Presley, was shown on a homemade screen outside on the open deck. As I watched from the stone wall that bordered the deck, I heard a very low rumble behind me, like distant thunder. When I turned to the sound, I saw Mama, her baby, and one of the juveniles in the dark, barely six feet from me, their stomachs rumbling.

RUMBLE RUMBLE

Apparently they were watching Elvis, too.

Perhaps the light and sound had drawn them to the movie. Maybe they had smelled the leftovers from dinner. Or maybe they just liked Elvis.

I held still, enjoying the closeness of such enormous wild creatures. Their stomachs continued to rumble. After a while they silently ambled away, past the DANGER, ELEPHANTS sign, and merged with the black tree line.

# AUTHOR'S NOTE

African elephants are found in forest and savanna areas south of the Sahara. They are even found in the desert in Namibia. African elephants are the largest land animals. They grow to a height of thirteen feet and can weigh up to thirteen thousand pounds, as much as three automobiles. Both males and females have tusks.

Elephants live in herds of ten to twenty animals led by an old female called a matriarch. Babies are born after a twenty-two month gestation period. They weigh two to three hundred pounds and are hairy at birth. The entire herd joins in the care and protection of the young.

Elephants love water and delight in bathing. To protect themselves from the sun and biting insects, they throw dirt over their backs. In doing so their gray color changes to the color of their habitat. Red dust, red elephants. They can live to be seventy years old. Elephants have few enemies except humans.

Murchison Falls National Park is the largest park in Uganda. Murchison Falls, one of the most amazing sights in Africa, feeds into the Victoria Nile, a river brimming with hippos and crocodiles. The park had been rich with plains animals until the 1970s and 1980s when poaching was at its heaviest. There were 15,000 elephants in the 1970s. Ten years later fewer than 200 remained. Now the park is home to more than 1,000 elephants, 20 species of predators, including lions, leopards, and side-striped jackals, and 460 species of birds. The comical-looking shoebill stork is found in its papyrus swamps.

Tiger track
(about ½ life-size)

# Glossary

*alder:* a northern deciduous shrub

*avens:* a perennial herb

*barnstormer:* a carnival stunt flyer

*bidi:* a dark, spicy cigarette

*bittern:* a North and South American wading bird with mottled plumage. A sun bittern has bright spots on its wings when extended.

*bog:* an area of soft, waterlogged ground

*booby:* a tropical seabird

*boreal forest:* a northern temperate forest of spruce, fir, and pine

*brand siekte:* a sunburnlike disease, which often results in death

*capybara:* a large South American semiaquatic grazing rodent

*carrion:* dead flesh

*chachalaca:* a large South American chickenlike bird

*clear-cut:* to cut down all the trees in a forest at one time

*cormorant:* a marine diving bird

*eland:* a very large African oxlike antelope with white stripes on the body

*fen:* low, flat swampy land

*gemsbok:* a large African antelope with striking "harness" pattern and long straight horns

*germinating:* sprouting

*gestation:* length of a pregnancy

*gimbal:* a device that allows an inclined object to remain level when it is tipped

*gully:* deep ditch cut by running water

*hacienda:* a house or small hotel

*hammock:* open expanse of high grass in a marshy region

*harem:* a group of females under the control of one large male

*hartebeest:* a large African antelope with a long face and sloping back

*howdah:* a wooden platform set on an elephant's back, used to carry passengers

*jacare:* a South American crocodile

*kestrel:* a small falcon

*kudu:* a large African antelope of the forest with stripes on the body and spiral horns

*lavu:* tipi

*lichen:* a fungus that grows in mutual dependence with algae, forming a crusty growth on rocks and tree trunks

*lynx:* a North American wildcat with a short tail and tufted ears

*mahout:* in India, a man who trains and cares for elephants

*mangrove:* a tropical evergreen tree with stiltlike roots

*muskeg:* a bog or marsh with thick layers of decaying vegetable matter, often overgrown with moss *pan:* a natural depression in the sand with a floor of hard clay

*panga:* a skiff; a small boat

*permafrost:* permanently frozen subsoil

*prehensile:* adapted for grasping

*ptarmigan:* an Arctic game bird

*rondavel:* a round house with a thatched roof

*scarab:* a kind of beetle

*souk:* open-air market

*tanager:* colorful North and South American forest birds

*tannic acid:* a chemical derived from the bark and fruit of many plants

*torrent:* a fast-flowing stream

*tuber:* underground stem or root

*tundra:* a treeless area in Arctic regions where the subsoil is
   permanently

# About the Author

Ted Lewin's love of wild animals began during his childhood, when he shared an old frame house in Buffalo, New York, with two brothers, one sister, two parents, a lion, an iguana, and a chimpanzee. After graduating from Pratt Institute, he combined his interest in exotic creatures with a passion for travel and art by illustrating for adventure magazines. His close encounters with wild animals of distant lands eventually inspired him to share his adventures with young readers.

Ted continues to travel. For the sequel to his popular book *Market!*, he haunted the floating markets of Thailand, bumping through crowded canals in a small boat. More recently he and his wife, Betsy Lewin, traveled to South America, braving the Andes and the Peruvian rain forest. In the near future Ted sets his sights on Mongolia, the South Seas, and the Pacific Northwest, where the mysterious totem poles surely hold stories for him to tell.

Ted is the illustrator of the Caldecott Honor Book *Peppe, the Lamplighter*. He is the author-illustrator of *Market!*, a *New York Times* Best Illustrated Book. *Gorilla Walk*, written and illustrated with his wife, was named a NSTA/CBC Outstanding Science Trade Book and an ALA Notable Book. Their second collaboration, *Elephant Quest*, was named a NSTA/CBC Outstanding Science Trade Book and received the 2000 John Burroughs Award (Outstanding Nature Book for Children).